I0606213

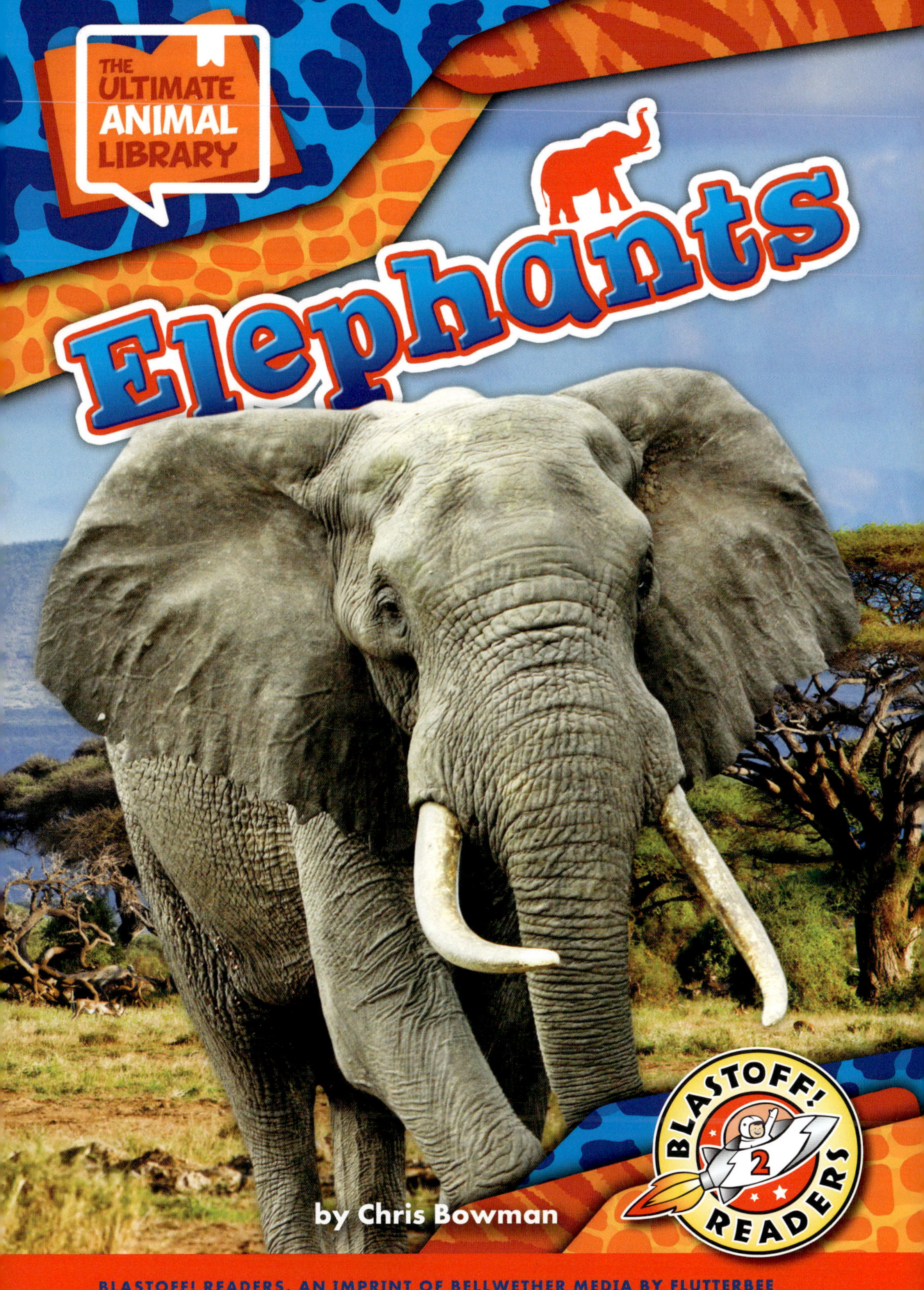

BLASTOFF! READERS, AN IMPRINT OF BELLWETHER MEDIA BY FLUTTERBEE

Blastoff! Readers are carefully developed by literacy experts to build reading stamina and move students toward fluency by combining standards-based content with developmentally appropriate text.

Level 1 provides the most support through repetition of high-frequency words, light text, predictable sentence patterns, and strong visual support.

Level 2 offers early readers a bit more challenge through varied sentences, increased text load, and text-supportive special features.

Level 3 advances early-fluent readers toward fluency through increased text load, less reliance on photos, advancing concepts, longer sentences, and more complex special features.

★ **Blastoff! Universe**

Reading Level

Grade K

Grades 1–3

Grade 4

This edition first published in 2026 by Bellwether Media, Inc.

For information regarding permission, write to Bellwether Media, Inc., Attention: Permissions Department, 3500 American Blvd W, Suite 150, Bloomington, MN 55431.

Library of Congress Cataloging-in-Publication Data is available at www.loc.gov or upon request from the publisher.

ISBN: 9798893047929 (hardcover)
ISBN: 9798893048926 (ebook)

Editor: Kieran Downs Designer: Brittany McIntosh

Printed in the United States of America, North Mankato, MN.

Table of Contents

What Are Elephants?

Elephants are the largest land animals in the world. These **mammals** live in Africa and Asia. There are three **species** of elephants.

African Bush Elephant Report

range =

Status in the Wild

endangered

Habitats

forests

swamps

savannas

grasslands

Elephants can weigh over 14,000 pounds (6,350 kilograms).

female

male

Males are bigger than females. They can be up to 13 feet (4 meters) tall.

Elephants use their long trunks to **communicate**. They make sounds that other elephants understand.

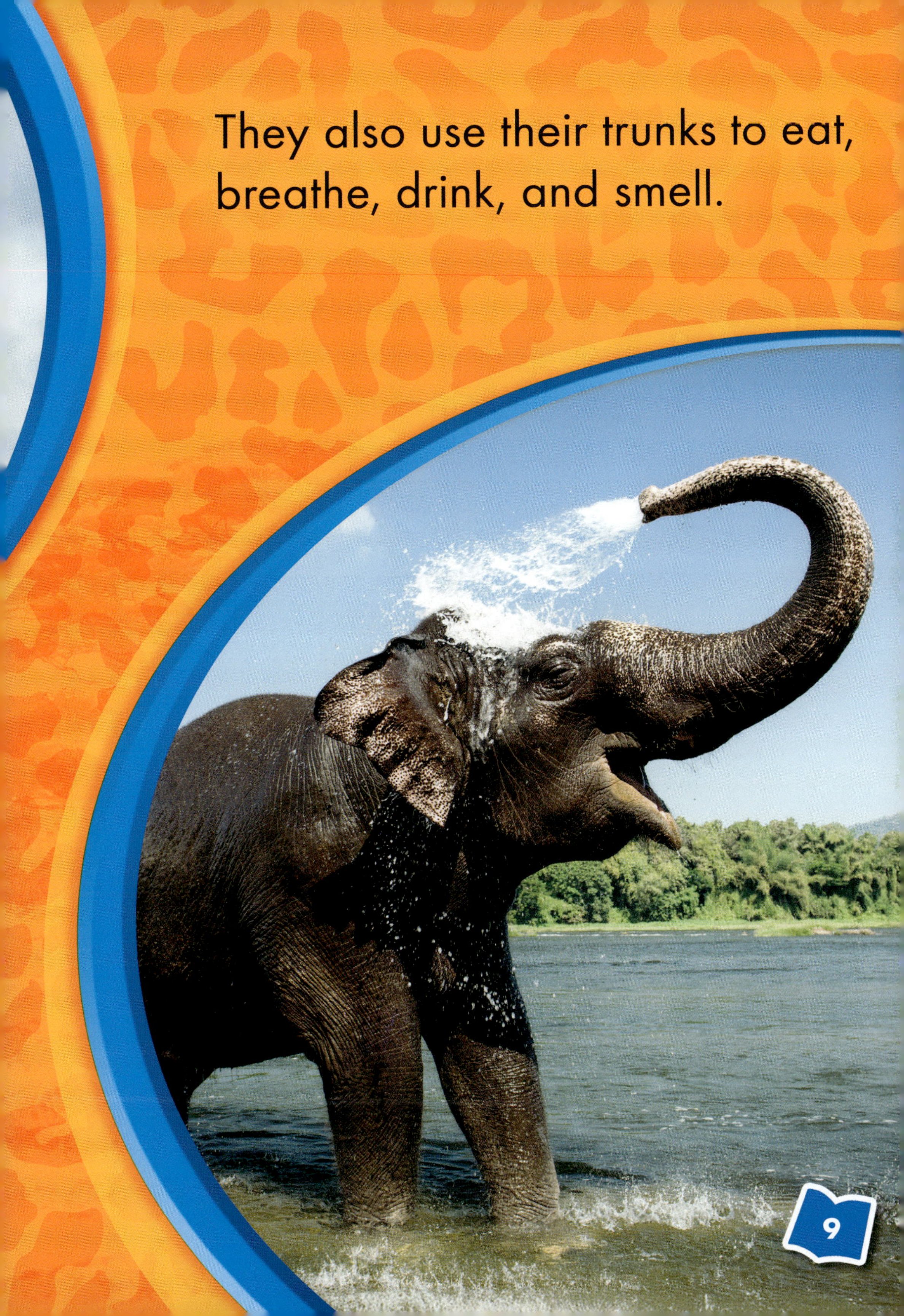

They also use their trunks to eat, breathe, drink, and smell.

Elephants have large ears. Many have long **tusks**.

Elephants have gray or brown skin. They have many **wrinkles**. They also have some hair.

Spot an Elephant
large ears
gray or brown skin
long trunk

Gentle Giants

Elephants live in forests and **swamps**. They can also be found in **savannas** and **grasslands**.

Females and young males live in **herds** of up to 70 elephants. Adult males often live alone or in small groups.

Elephants are **herbivores**. They eat fruits and leaves. They also eat bark and twigs.

Shrubs and grasses also make a quick snack.

Elephants do not have many **predators** due to their size.

But they are sometimes hunted
by predators such as lions.

Growing Up

Female elephants usually give birth to one **calf** at a time. They have a calf about once every five years.

Calves **nurse** for up to six years.

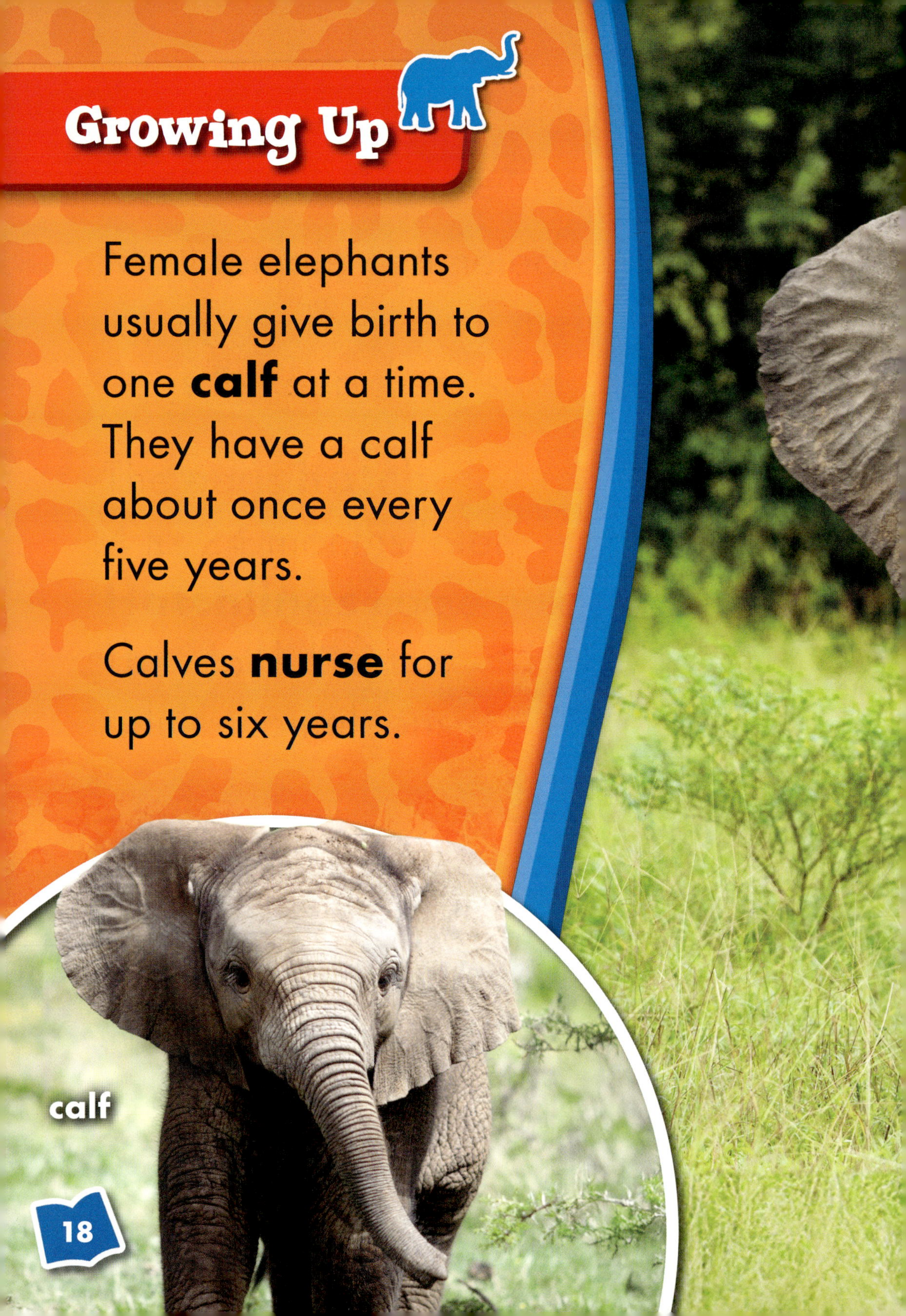

calf

Calves grow up with their herds. After around 10 years, males go off on their own.

Females stay in their herds. Time to care for new calves!

Life of an Elephant

Name of Babies

calves

Number of Babies

1

Time Spent with Mom

around 10 years

Life Span

up to 70 years

Glossary

calf—a baby elephant

communicate—to share information and feelings

grasslands—lands covered with grasses and other soft plants with few bushes or trees

herbivores—animals that only eat plants

herds—groups of animals that live and travel together

mammals—warm-blooded animals that have backbones and feed their young milk

nurse—to drink mom's milk

predators—animals that hunt other animals for food

savannas—flat grasslands with few trees

species—kinds of an animal

swamps—wetlands filled with trees and other woody plants

tusks—the long, pointed teeth of elephants

wrinkles—folds or creases

To Learn More

AT THE LIBRARY

Duling, Kaitlyn. *African Elephants.* Minneapolis, Minn.: Bellwether Media, 2020.

Grack, Rachel. *Elephants.* Minneapolis, Minn.: Bellwether Media, 2022.

Sabelko, Rebecca. *Grassland Animals.* Minneapolis, Minn.: Bellwether Media, 2023.

ON THE WEB

FACTSURFER

Factsurfer.com gives you a safe, fun way to find more information.

1. Go to www.factsurfer.com.
2. Enter "elephants" into the search box and click 🔍.
3. Select your book cover to see a list of related content.

Index

The images in this book are reproduced through the courtesy of: Talvi, front cover (elephant); PHOTOCREO Michal Bednarek, front cover (background), pp. 2-3; Vibe Images, p. 3; Henk Bogaard, pp. 4, 13; Decha Kiatlatchanon, p. 6; Danita Delimont Creative, p. 7; AndreAnita, p. 8; Dmytro Gilitukha, p. 9; Wirestock, p. 10; Maksym Gorpenyuk, pp. 10-11; Nancy Pauwels, p. 11; hangingpixels, p. 12; ISSARAPONG KANTHAROD, pp. 14-15; jirihosko, p. 15 (lions); Villiers Steyn, p. 15 (elephant); nutt, p. 15 (fruits); ESstock, p. 15 (leaves); larisa Stefanjuk, p. 15 (bark); Sourabh Bharti, p. 16; Jez Bennett, p. 17; JONATHAN PLEDGER, p. 18; Johan W. Elzenga, pp. 18-19; Tero Vesalainen, p. 20; worradirek, p. 21; Martin Gallie, p. 23.